Snap books®

# PERSEPHONE

## GREEK GODDESS OF THE UNDERWORLD

by Amie Jane Leavitt

Content Consultant
Susan C. Shelmerdine, PhD,
Professor of Classical Studies
University of North Carolina, Greensboro
Greensboro, NC

CAPSTONE PRESS
a capstone imprint

Snap Books are published by Capstone Press,
1710 Roe Crest Drive, North Mankato, Minnesota 56003
www.mycapstone.com

**Library of Congress Cataloging-in-Publication Data**
Names: Leavitt, Amie Jane, author.
Title: Persephone: Greek goddess of the underworld / by Amie Jane Leavitt.
Description: North Mankato: Capstone Press, 2019. | Series: Snap Books.
   Legendary goddesses | Includes index.
Identifiers: LCCN 2018036726| ISBN 9781543554540 (library binding) |
ISBN   9781543559170 (pbk.) | ISBN 9781543554588 (ebook pdf)
Subjects:  LCSH: Persephone (Greek deity)—Juvenile literature.
Classification: LCC BL820.P7 L43 2019 | DDC 292.2/114—dc23
LC record available at https://lccn.loc.gov/2018036726

**Editorial Credits**
Gina Kammer, editor
Bobbie Nuytten, designer
Svetlana Zhurkin, media researcher
Katy LaVigne, production specialist

**Image Credits**
Alamy: Hackenberg-Photo-Cologne, cover, History and Art Collection, 8, Sklifas
Steven, 27 (bottom), World Archive, 26; Getty Images: Heritage Images/Fine
Art Images, 12, UIG/Picturenow, 10; Newscom: akg-images, 22, Album/Imprint
Entertainment/Fox 2000 Pictures/1492 Pictures, 29, Liszt Collection, 19 (bottom),
World History Archive, 14; North Wind Picture Archives, 7; Shutterstock: Africa
Studio, 25, Andrey Khusnutdinov, 19 (top), Iasen Doltshinkov, 15 (top),
Masterrr, 20, Ratikova, 17, Samot, 28, Theastock, 15 (middle and bottom),
vectortatu, 11; Svetlana Zhurkin, 4, 16, 18, 27 (top); Wikimedia: Wikipedia
Saves Public Art, 24

Design Elements by Shutterstock

# TABLE OF CONTENTS

# Chapter 1

# THE SEASONS COME TO ANCIENT GREECE

Persephone was the Greek goddess of the spring. One of the main myths about Persephone tells the story of how she became queen of the **underworld**.

Cotton clouds clung to the **cypress** slopes of Mount Olympus. Golden fields ripe with grain stood ready for harvest. It was just another stunning day for the Olympic **pantheon**, the gods who ruled over ancient Greece. On this delightful morning, Zeus sat in his cloud palace overseeing his kingdom. Suddenly, his brother, Hades, stormed into the room.

Persephone was the beautiful goddess of spring growth and of the sprouting of seeds.

4

"Zeus, I need to speak with you," Hades bellowed. The god who ruled in the **underworld** bowed at Zeus's feet. "I have come to ask for your daughter Persephone's hand in marriage," he continued. "I have been watching her as she picks flowers in the fields. I know she will make me very happy."

"Have you spoken to her about this?" Zeus asked.

"No. I knew Demeter would never allow me to marry her daughter," Hades explained.

"Well, Persephone is my daughter too," said Zeus. "And I am the king of the gods. Persephone could find no better match than to marry my brother. You have my permission."

Hades' dark appearance lit up in a fiery glow. "I must hurry to make my plans," he said, as he rushed out of the palace.

## GODDESS FACT

The earliest, lengthy version of Persephone's story that still exists is the *Hymn to Demeter*. It was a poem written sometime around 650 BC.

**cypress**—a type of evergreen tree
**pantheon**—all the gods of a particular mythology
**underworld**—the world of the dead or of the spirits

At the base of Mount Olympus, Persephone and her mother, Demeter, walked through the golden fields. They often visited the farmers of ancient Greece and helped them with their crops. This was their most important job. They knew that the farmers needed a productive harvest. Otherwise they would have little to sacrifice to the Olympic pantheon. Small sacrifices always angered Zeus and the other gods. To keep the peace, Demeter, goddess of agriculture, and Persephone, goddess of springtime, made sure the crops were always good and plentiful.

"Mother, I want to pick some flowers for you," Persephone said as they walked through a field of creamy **narcissus**.

"You may pick the flowers, my daughter," Demeter gave her permission. "I will be nearby with the farmers."

Persephone soaked in the sunshine as she picked her bouquet. She was nearly finished when she suddenly heard a terrible rumbling sound from deep within the earth. Just steps in front of her, the earth cracked open like a bursting volcano. Out of the dark gap rushed Hades. He was on his golden **chariot** pulled by a team of ebony black horses. Before Persephone could catch her breath, Hades had her locked in his grip. He whisked her away into the darkness below.

"Mother!" Persephone shrieked as the earth sealed tightly over them.

Demeter dropped the stalk of grain she was checking and rushed toward her daughter's cries. Yet, all she found was the bouquet of narcissus scattered on the ground. Persephone's footprints were still fresh in the soft soil.

"Persephone!" Demeter wailed. Her voice vibrated every blade of grass on earth.

But there was no reply. Demeter hunted the planet. She turned up every rock. She looked behind every tree. She invaded every mountain cave. But it was of no use. Persephone was nowhere to be found.

narcissus—a flower that resembles the daffodil with white or pale colored outer petals and yellow or orange inner petals

chariot—a light, two-wheeled cart pulled by horses

Hades steals Persephone away on his chariot to the underworld. In the oldest myths, this event happened near Athens.

The months dragged on and the earth began to suffer. Through her grief, Demeter no longer helped the farmers with their crops. Her Persephone was gone. Demeter no longer cared about anything. There was no life for her without Persephone.

Demeter mourns the loss of her daughter, Persephone. Meanwhile, nothing grew for the people on earth to eat.

Zeus knew he had to take action or the entire earth would be destroyed. He sent his son Hermes into the underworld with his winged sandals to retrieve Persephone. Zeus ordered that the deal with Hades had to be off. No marriage was worth the earth's destruction.

When Hermes arrived in the dark caverns of the underworld, though, he discovered he was too late. Persephone had fallen in love with Hades after she had eaten some of Hades' pomegranate seeds.

"Because she has dined in the underworld," Hades defiantly explained, "she can never return to earth. That is the law of the gods." Hermes relayed the message to Zeus.

"Some rules are made to be broken!" Zeus shouted at Hades from the top of Mount Olympus. In his anger, the king of the gods sent lightning bolts sizzling across the sky. "You may have her for one part of the year, Hades. But during the rest of the year, she must return to her mother on earth."

Persephone felt happy about this agreement. She did love Hades. But she loved her mother too. Now, she would get to be the goddess of springtime and help save the earth. And she'd also get to sit on the throne next to her husband and reign as the queen of the underworld.

Demeter was overjoyed when Persephone returned. The earth turned green again. Flowers sprang up wherever Persephone stepped. The crops in the field were plentiful, just as they had always been before. When the harvest was over, Demeter cried again when Persephone had to leave. The plants dried up. The fruit withered. And the earth went silent for the winter. But then in the spring every year, the cycle repeated when all came to life once again when Persephone reunited with her adoring mother.

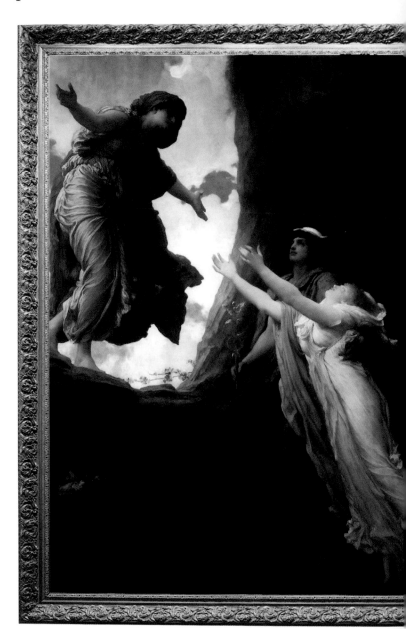

Persephone returns to her mother, Demeter, from the underworld.

# Explaining Natural Events

The ancient Greeks weren't the only people to invent myths to explain natural events. Many ancient cultures did the same. Back in ancient times, people didn't have today's scientific evidence and theories to explain such things as night and day, the change of seasons, the tides, the constellations, and moon phases. So making up stories about gods and goddesses or animal characters was one way they could make sense of what they saw in the world around them.

According to Native American Cherokee legends, the seasons changed every year because a nature god cursed the leafy trees that refused to help a wounded bird. In ancient China, people believed that the earth had four seasons because a fire breathing dragon in a mountain warmed and cooled the air. And in South America, the people believed that a cloud god decided to form the seasons as a way to end a quarrel between the animals.

# Chapter 2

# A PRINCESS IS BORN

The ancient Greeks worshipped many gods and goddesses. They made up stories, or myths, that explained how the deities came to be and how they impacted life on earth. At first, the Greeks worshipped the Titans. But then the Titans lost a mythical battle to their children, the Olympians. After the Olympic pantheon seized control, the ancient Greeks started worshipping these new gods. The great Olympian god Zeus was the new supreme ruler. In this role, he was the king of the gods.

The Olympian gods had cloud palaces on beautiful Mount Olympus. Twelve of the gods sat together on a grand council just as twelve Titan gods once reigned.

A painting in the Palazzo Pitti in Florence, Italy, shows the Greek gods ruling together on Olympus.

Each **deity** ruled over a different part of the kingdom. Zeus ruled the sky. He used his famous thunderbolt to electrify the heavens during lightning storms. Poseidon commanded the seas by wielding his powerful three-pronged **trident**. Hades reigned the underworld and rode his black-horsed golden chariot. Demeter was the goddess of agriculture. She was much beloved by the humans because she provided them with plenty to eat and abundant harvests in their fields.

# THE 12 OLYMPIANS

**ZEUS** - king of the gods and god of the sky
**DEMETER** - goddess of agriculture
**ARTEMIS** - goddess of hunting
**ATHENA** - goddess of wisdom and war
**DIONYSUS** - god of wine
**HEPHAISTOS** - god of fire and the **forge**
**HERA** - queen of the gods and goddess of marriage
**HERMES** - messenger and god of trade
**POSEIDON** - god of the sea
**APHRODITE** - goddess of love and beauty
**APOLLO** - god of music
**ARES** - god of war

*Hades is sometimes considered one of the Twelve Olympians instead of Hephaistos.*

**deity**—god or goddess
**trident**—a long spear with three sharp points at its end
**forge**—the special furnace in which metal is heated to be formed

# WELCOMING SPRING

The gods and goddesses had many offspring together. One sunny, green day on Mount Olympus, a tiny new baby was born to Zeus and Demeter. Since the baby was the daughter of gods, she was also a goddess and a princess. They named her Persephone. She became the goddess of springtime.

Demeter cared for Persephone, and the two were always together.

Princess Persephone was Demeter's only daughter with Zeus. Demeter adored Persephone and thought she was the most beautiful child ever to be born. Mother and daughter spent most of their time together. They often roamed the fields on earth and visited the farmers to check on their crops. Everywhere Persephone stepped, colorful flowers and tiny new plants would spring to life along her path.

If Persephone was considered beautiful as a child, then she was gorgeous as a young woman. But Demeter sheltered Persephone, wanting to keep her safe. Even so, many of the gods began to notice her loveliness and said she was more stunning than any of the earth's plants or flowers. Persephone, however, was still young and wasn't interested in any of them. That was until she met Hades.

## Mount Olympus

Mount Olympus is a real place. It's actually the highest mountain in all of Greece. It rises about 9,570 feet (2,917 meters) above sea level. Because it soared high into the heavens, it was natural for the ancient Greeks to choose this location as the seat of their gods.

Today, many people like to climb to the top of Mount Olympus. Along the way, they marvel at how green much of it is and how many kinds of plants are found there. Mount Olympus has more than 1,700 different species of plants. Some of these species are only found in Greece, and some are found nowhere else but Mount Olympus.

**••••• GODDESS FACT •••••**

Persephone is also called Kore meaning "maiden." Some myths say she took the name Persephone after she became queen of the underworld.

# Chapter 3

# A ROYAL FAMILY

Persephone had royal blood surging through her veins. Not only was she the daughter of two Olympian gods, she was also the granddaughter of Titan gods.

Zeus and Demeter were both the children of the Titan god Cronus and the Titan goddess Rhea. Cronus and Rhea were the children of Uranus and Gaia, who were Father Sky and Mother Earth. So, by just going back to her great-grandparents, Persephone could stretch her **lineage** all the way back to the beginning days of the Greek universe.

Uranus and Gaia were Persephone's great-grandparents.

## ROYALTY ABOUNDS

Persephone had a big extended family with many famous aunts and uncles including Hera, Poseidon, and Hestia. Hades was also part of her extended family too. He was her father's oldest brother.

Zeus and Demeter had many children with other gods. This gave Persephone many half-brothers and half-sisters. Some examples are Athena, the goddess of war, and Aphrodite, the goddess of love, who were half-sisters on her father's side. Hermes, the winged-sandaled god who came to rescue her from the underworld, was her half-brother on the same side. On her mother's side, Despoina, Plutus, Philomelus, and Arion, the winged horse, were her half-siblings.

## ·····• GODDESS FACT •·····

Most of the Greek deities had perfectly shaped human bodies, but they also had the power to change forms. They often made themselves look like other humans, or they took on the shape of animals like horses, serpents, bulls, swans, and eagles.

**lineage**—ancestry or heritage

# PERSEPHONE'S OFFSPRING

Persephone had one daughter. Her name was Melinoe. Since she was born in the underworld, she became the goddess of ghosts. Every night, Melinoe would haunt the earth with a pack of ghosts trailing behind her. Her goal was to terrorize humankind. She aimed to spook every human who crossed her path.

Melinoe was the goddess of ghosts and wandered the earth inspiring fear in humans.

Persephone also had a son named Zagreus. He was another god of the underworld. According to the myths, he and Melinoe were the children of Zeus, not Hades. In the legends, Zeus disguised himself as Hades in order to trick Persephone into falling for him. This resulted in the birth of Melinoe. Zeus also turned himself into a snake to trick Persephone, and together they had Zagreus.

## GODDESS FACT

The snake carries many different symbols for ancient cultures. In ancient Greece, the snake was a symbol for eternity. Thus, the snake would have been appealing to Persephone.

## Unusual Family Ties

How could Zeus and Demeter be brother and sister *and* the parents of Persephone? How can Persephone's grandparents and great-grandparents be siblings, too? Why did Persephone marry her uncle and have a son with her father? The answer can be summed up in one sentence: the mythical deities were make-believe beings and therefore lived under their own standards and laws.

In Greek mythology, gods and goddesses in the same family frequently married or had children together. According to the myths, this allowed the deities to pass on their special superhuman powers to their offspring.

Hera and Zeus were also siblings who married. Athena stands between them on this vase.

# Persephone's family tree

The goddess of the underworld was the daughter of Zeus and Demeter. Persephone had many half-siblings from each of them in her family tree. Persephone married Hades, god of the underworld, and had two children of her own, Melinoe and Zagreus, with Zeus.

*The king of the gods was Persephone's father.*

**ZEUS**

**DEMETER**

**PERSEPHONE**

*The goddess of agriculture was Persephone's mother.*

**RHEA**

*The god of the dead and the underworld married Persephone.*

**HADES**

**CRONUS**

···· Grandparents
···· Parents
···· Siblings
···· Children

**Melinoe**

*Persephone's children with Zeus*

**Zagreus**

**ATHENA**

**APHRODITE**

**ARES**

**APOLLO**

**HERMES**

*some of Persephone's half-siblings on her father's (Zeus's) side*

**DESPOINA**

**PLUTUS**

**PHILOMELUS**

**ARION**

*some of Persephone's half-siblings on her mother's (Demeter's) side*

# Chapter 4

# PERSEPHONE'S DUAL PERSONALITY

As goddess of springtime, Persephone has special powers over the plants, flowers, and soil. Her very footsteps cause life to suddenly appear. The ancient Greeks believed that her arrival from the underworld every spring caused the earth to spring to life. When she left after autumn, the plants withered and died and the earth went dormant for winter.

Persephone was fated to stay in the underworld after she had eaten the pomegranate seeds given to her by Hades. Only Zeus could allow Persephone to return for part of the year.

Persephone has dual personalities. She looks different as goddess of springtime than she does as queen of the underworld. As goddess of springtime, Persephone has flowing golden hair crowned with a wreath of lilies, daisies, and lavender. She often holds reeds, grain, and narcissus in her hands.

As queen of the underworld, Persephone has a darker appearance. Her satiny hair, now a deep black or auburn, is decorated with a golden crown. In one hand, Queen Persephone carries a ruby red pomegranate. In the other, she holds a fiery torch to light her way through the dark underworld.

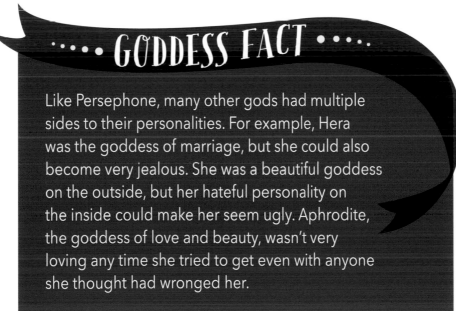

## GODDESS FACT

Like Persephone, many other gods had multiple sides to their personalities. For example, Hera was the goddess of marriage, but she could also become very jealous. She was a beautiful goddess on the outside, but her hateful personality on the inside could make her seem ugly. Aphrodite, the goddess of love and beauty, wasn't very loving any time she tried to get even with anyone she thought had wronged her.

# PERSEPHONE'S RESPONSIBILITIES

On earth, Persephone's role is to bring life. In the underworld, she serves as a guide or hostess to the dead as they make their way through the land of the spirits. Thus, she has both life-giving and care-giving roles. Because of that, she doesn't have any need for weapons. She doesn't have a thunderbolt like her father, Zeus. She has no need for a trident to command the seas and storms, like her uncle Poseidon. She doesn't need winged sandals or a headdress like Hermes or an invisible helmet like Hades. Persephone is more like her mother. They are both peaceful goddesses who do not carry any kind of arms to use for protection or revenge.

## GODDESS FACT

A bronze statue of Persephone stands on the grounds of Butler University in Indianapolis. It was created in Paris by the French sculptor Armand Toussaint in 1840 to symbolize the growth and life that come with the goddess's return from the underworld. It has been in the university gardens since 1950.

# An Important Ancient Symbol

In plants, seeds are necessary for reproduction. The more seeds a plant produces, the greater chance the plant has to survive, especially in harsh climates. Pomegranates are filled with hundreds of seeds. Thus, this fruit represented birth, rebirth, eternal life, and marriage to ancient peoples.

The ancient Greeks weren't the only ones to see the pomegranate as significant. This ruby red fruit with its juicy seeds was also an important symbol for many other cultures (Persian and Chinese) and religions (Islamic, Hebrew, Hindu, and Christian), too. Even today, the pomegranate is still important in Greek festivals and celebrations.

# Chapter 5

# LIVING FOREVER

Persephone was an important goddess for the ancient Greek people. People who depended on agriculture for their livelihood especially worshipped her and her mother. Farmers believed that properly worshipping these goddesses would help them have rich harvests.

The ancients often had special festivals to honor these goddesses. One was the Thesmophoria. This festival was held in the fall every year. Generally, only women were allowed to participate in the festival. During the three-day event, the women dressed in creamy-white tunics. They traveled together by foot to the event site. They prayed to Demeter and Persephone and offered sacrifices to them. They also provided various entertainment to make Demeter laugh. If she was happy, the plants would grow the next spring. This celebration may have included remembering the myths of how Persephone was about to return from the underworld.

Another festival was held in the fall called the Eleusinian Mysteries. All could attend. This festival was connected to the story of how Hades captured Persephone to be his wife.

The Greek people celebrate Thesmophoria and bring sacrifices. They offered the first fruits of the harvest to the gods.

## SYMBOLS OF PERSEPHONE

golden crown

torch

pomegranate

# Roman Mythology and Persephone

The Greeks weren't the only ones who worshipped Persephone. The Romans also worshipped her as the goddess of spring and queen of the underworld. In Roman mythology, Persephone was also kidnapped by Hades. However, in the Roman version, she is known as Proserpina and he is known as Pluto.

# THE GREEK GODS TODAY

Only a small number of people in Greece today still worship the Olympic Pantheon. Those who do follow the Hellenismos religion and are called Hellenes or Hellenists. They study the classical writings about the gods. They respect the ancient Greek **temples** as holy places. They live by a code of ethics. They try to be humble, live in moderation, and have self-control. They celebrate the traditional festivals like the ancients always did. They pray to the gods and make sacrifices to them.

Greek mythology has had a wide influence in the culture of the western world for thousands of years. Even today, people are still influenced by these ancient gods and legends. Authors, artists, musicians, and moviemakers have all been inspired by these age-old tales.

temple ruins at Delphi, an ancient Greek city.

It doesn't matter if one believes that a god can be **immortal** or not. The fact that the stories of the Olympic pantheon have lived on for as long as they have certainly says something. It shows that even if it's just through art, these gods will live on forever!

> **immortal**—able to live forever
> **temple**—a building used for worship

## Persephone in Pop Culture

Persephone has had a wide influence on modern pop culture. For example, an Amazonian warrior in the 2009 *Wonder Woman* film is named Persephone. Best-selling author Stephen King named one of his characters Perse, short for Persephone, in his book *Duma Key*. Numerous video games either have characters and places named after Persephone, such as in *Skylanders*. Or they have used the overall story idea of Persephone's kidnapping as their plot line. There are also dozens of books and movies with Persephone-inspired plots, characters, and themes. Even musicians and playwrights have based works on the queen of the underworld.

### GODDESS FACT

Persephone is one of the goddesses featured in two of Rick Riordan's Percy Jackson titles: *The Demigod Files* and *The Last Olympian*.

# GLOSSARY

**chariot** (CHAYR-ee-uht)—a light, two-wheeled cart pulled by horses

**cypress** (SYE-pruhs)—a type of evergreen tree

**deity** (DEE-uh-tee)—god or goddess

**forge** (FORJ)—the special furnace in which metal is heated to be formed

**immortal** (i-MOR-tuhl)—able to live forever

**lineage** (LIN-ee-aje)—ancestry or heritage

**narcissus** (nar-SISS-uhs)—a flower that resembles the daffodil with white or pale colored outer petals and yellow or orange inner petals

**pantheon** (PAN-thee-on)—all the gods of a particular mythology

**temple** (TEM-puhl)—a building used for worship

**trident** (TRY-dent)—a long spear with three sharp points at its end

**underworld** (UHN-dur-wurld)—the world of the dead or of the spirits

# READ MORE

**Braun, Eric**. *Greek Myths. Mythology Around the World.* North Mankato, Minn.: Capstone Press, 2019.

**Lupton, Hugh**. *Greek Myths: Three Heroic Tales.* Cambridge, Mass.: Barefoot Books, 2017.

**Hoena, Blake**. *Everything Mythology.* Washington, D. C.: National Geographic, 2014.

# INTERNET SITES

Use FactHound to find Internet sites related to this book.

Visit *www.facthound.com*

Just type in 9781543554540 and go!

 Check out projects, games and lots more at
**www.capstonekids.com**

# INDEX